# Preachers
# Priests

# and
# Critters

# Preachers
# Priests

# and
# Critters

And other
unusual accounts

Edited by Eric Mills

HORIZON HOUSE PUBLISHERS
Box 600
Beaverlodge, Alberta, Canada

ISBN O-88965-003-9

**HORIZON BOOKS**
are published by Horizon House Publishers
Box 600, Beaverlodge, Alberta, Canada TOH OCO
Printed in the United States of America

## *Dedication*

To Keith and Alice Lonie, who have loved Camp
Nakamun and labored long to extend its ministry
around the world, this volume of Camp-Meeting
Cream is affectionately dedicated.

# Contents

# Introduction

You have just picked up an unusual collection of materials that were first given orally at summer camps, then printed in our periodical, **Communicate**. If you have ever heard about brush-arbor revivals, sawdust trails, and camp meetings, you may have wondered what is said under those tents and tabernacles that religious people still erect.

This book gives you a chance to breathe that atmosphere. (You may even smell the sawdust!) Certainly you will sense the excitement. There is a romance about the old-time religion in a rustic setting. Some of the talks are highly entertaining. There's laughter too. And perhaps a few tears.

But we have felt that what we call "camp-meeting cream" had somehow to find a larger audience. Eric Mills, book editor for Horizon House, has done a fine job of editing the tumbling words of spoken speech. The result is Camp-Meeting Cream, Vol. 1. You'll enjoy it, we know. And keep watching the bookstores. It is probably just the first of a series.

K. Neill Foster
Horizon House Publishers

# Preachers, Priests, and Critters

## by Rev. Jimmie Bersche

MY FATHER was a saloon-keeper and a drunkard. Our living quarters were connected to his saloon. As a result, I learned to drink beer when I was knee-high to a duck.

My father taught us kids, "Children, the worst creatures God ever let live are priests and preachers. The very ground on which these critters walk is contaminated. If you see one of them coming up the road, cross over to the road's other side and spit in contempt."

Naturally, being an obedient son, I always did what my dad said!

Well, God had other ideas for my family and me. He began to work out those ideas by giving my mother a job in which she was to work beside a tremendous Christian woman. One day, this woman asked Mom to go with her to church, a church where they believed and preached the Bible. Mom went and was gloriously converted to Jesus Christ. Her life was wonderfully changed and she later led many people to faith in Jesus. That was step one!

God's second step was moving my family and me to Kentucky. For it was in Kentucky that a boyhood friend one day said to me, "I'd like to have you go with me to a protracted meeting." (Until then, I'd never heard of such a thing, but I learned that a "protracted meeting" is a series of church meetings which begins on a certain date and continues indefinitely.)

Well, when I found out that a "protracted meeting" was a church service, I said, "No way! I'm not going to sit there and listen to one of those critters!" And I told my friend what my dad had told me about preachers.

He said, "I've never heard anybody talk about preachers like **that**! But you know what? Around here, all the young people look forward to protracted meetings. Because a protracted meeting is the best place around here to meet girls!" He was a good salesman—I went.

But I surely didn't know what I was in for! It was an old-fashioned, "shouting Methodist" church, complete with "Amen corner." And the more the people shouted, the better the preacher preached! And the worse I felt.

He got on that sin bit. He told those people every sin I'd ever done. And just so they'd know who he was talking about, he kept pointing his finger at me! I was scared half to death he'd holler, "Jimmy Bersche, I'm talking about **you**!"

And I fell under deep, deep conviction. Night after night, I was afraid to go to sleep for fear that while I was unconscious I might slip into hell.

12

Finally, on the tenth night of meetings, I walked to the front of that church and was "born again" of the Holy Spirit. I was changed completely in a moment. And I knew I was called to be one of those "critters" known as preachers.

A year later, there was a major family problem in our home and our family scattered to the four winds. I went to Detroit with one purpose in mind: to get a job to make some money to go to school to become a preacher. I left home with seventy-five dollars, a dilapidated handbag, two pairs of overalls, and a Sunday suit. I was seventeen years old.

When I arrived in Detroit, I tried to find a job. But everywhere I went, the answer was the same: "We need **skilled** labor." Without a skill to offer, it seemed there just wasn't a job to be found. That continued for weeks.

One day I returned to my boarding house to find a telegram awaiting me. It said: "Have not heard from you. Dad is much better. Not necessary to return. Glen." Glen was my brother. The rest was a mystery. I had no idea what he was talking about.

After supper, another telegram arrived. This one said: "Dad blown up in powder plant. Not expected to live. Return at once. Glen."

As I compared the dates on the two telegrams, I noted an important detail: the telegram that I had received second had been sent first. It had been delayed for two days.

If I had received that first telegram sent when I theoretically should have received it, I'd have borrowed some money and headed home to talk to my father before he died. And once at home, I'd have never made it back to Detroit.

But my heavenly Father knew my dad wasn't going

13

to die. And because His blueprint called for me to remain in Detroit, He worked it so that I would remain in Detroit!

One night in the rooming house, one of the men asked, "How old are you?"

I said, "I'm seventeen."

"You can't get a job up here if you're only seventeen. You've got to be at least twenty-one. You'd better say you're twenty-five."

Well, I was tempted. The devil said, "It's okay to tell a little lie. After all, it's so you can become a preacher!"

But that night as I talked with my heavenly Father I decided I must tell the truth. Job or no job.

One day, about 4:45 P.M., I came to a small factory. I walked in and asked for a job. The employment officer gave me the same old answer: "Sorry, we want skilled labor."

Discouraged, I turned for the door. And then the officer called, "Wait a minute! A card came in an hour or two ago. It's for an apprentice in the tool room. You could do that!"

"I'll take it!" I said.

Then, looking at his watch, the employment officer announced, "It's almost quitting time. Come back tomorrow and I'll look after the application forms."

"Please sir," I said, "couldn't I get started at the job tomorrow?"

And so he picked up his phone, talked a minute, and finally said, "All right. The foreman wants someone tomorrow. Take this badge and he'll pick you up. I'll give you the forms a little later in the morning."

I've lived around industrial areas most of my Christian life. I've never, ever known one person to get into one of those places without completing those forms. But I did! You see, God had it in His plan.

If I'd have arrived at that employment office a few minutes earlier, the employment officer would have thrown those forms at me and after filling in my age, I'd have been a dead duck. Seeing how young I was, the officer would have immediately said, "Sorry, you're too young to work here." (As it was, I got into the plant without being **asked** my age!)

By the time the foreman learned I was only seventeen, I was already on the job. He came to me and said, "Son, if I'd have known you were only seventeen, I'd have never brought you into the plant. And certainly not into the tool room. All this machinery—if anything happened to you, your parents could sue this factory for thousands of dollars. You can finish the day, but that is all you can work here."

Looking back, I think that day was one of the darkest days of my life. Disillusioned, no parents to turn to, no Christian friends, I felt as though God had forsaken me. And the devil jumped on my shoulder and screamed that I was a fool for not lying about my age.

An hour before quitting time, the foreman came up to me and said, "I don't know why I've done this for you. But I've been all over this factory trying to find you a job. And you know, it just so happens that up on the top floor where they wrap and assemble the valves, a man was fired this afternoon. The only people up there now are a blind man and a bunch of girls. If it's safe for them, it ought to be safe for a kid of seventeen! You can work up there!"

Oh, that didn't "just so happen!" It was all a part of a wonderful blueprint—God's perfect plan for me.

15

The next day, I decided to eat my lunch with the blind man, whose name was George. (Since all of the "girls" were at least as old as my mother, I didn't want to eat lunch with them!) After we'd gotten blind George's lunch laid out, George simply said, "Jimmie, I always pray before I eat." And he started to talk to Jesus.

And when George did that, I almost choked. You see, blind George's name was on the blueprint. He was waiting there all along.

And I could have missed blind George. If the first telegram sent had been the first telegram received, I'd have been living down in southern Illinois, not Detroit. If I'd have lied about my age, I'd have been down in the tool room, not up in the wrapping and assembling area where I would meet blind George.

God knew all of that all along. And He knew that a little country kid in a big city needed a spiritual father. And He led me to George.

In the mornings before work began, George and I would spend some time together each day. At our lunch times, George would talk to me about Christ. And for me, that factory became a very exciting, profitable place!

One day George said, "Jimmie, I've been meaning to ask you, son, where do you go to church?"

I replied, "George, I've only recently started attending church here in Detroit. And I've started to go to the Protestant church near my boarding house...." (You see, at that time I thought all Protestant churches were the same.)

"What's the church's name, son?"

So I told him and he said, "Oh, they don't even believe in the virgin birth! They surely don't believe in being born again, or converted. Jimmie, you've

16

got to find a church where they believe and preach the Bible."

"George, where do **you** go to church?" I asked.

He said, "Why, I go to the Christian and Missionary Alliance." And the Christian and Missionary Alliance became my church, too.

Well, somewhere along the line I wrote my mom and dad and brothers and sister and told them, "Come on up to Detroit. There's work for all of you!" (You see, unlike me, they had some skills to offer.) And, in due course, the whole Bersche tribe came to Detroit. This, too, was a part of God's plan, as you'll see in a minute.

One day the Alliance preacher came to me and said, "Jimmie, I got something in the mail today. They're beginning a Bible school at Beulah Beach. I believe this is the time for you to apply to go to Bible school."

By then I had some money saved, and I applied and was accepted. I began making plans to go to school in September.

When it came time for me to leave, the pastor said, "Jimmie, I want you to preach on Sunday night before you leave."

"Pastor, I'd be glad to," I replied. (I'd never actually "preached" in all my life!) I went back to the boarding house my mom operated and I said to my dad, brothers, cousins, and the other men, "I'm going to preach on Sunday night. I'd like you all to be there."

And you know, come Sunday night, they all were there! And others were, too. In fact, when I got up to preach that night, our little church was full.

Well, I didn't really preach at all. I just told the people some of the things I've been telling you. I told

17

them about the two telegrams—and there was my brother, Glen, sittting there. I told them about the explosion that almost killed my father—and there was my father sitting somewhere at the back. I told them about meeting blind George—and he and his wife were sitting about three rows from the front. And as I told them how wonderful God was to have given me George Sieber as my spiritual father, I couldn't do it without emotion, because that man meant so much to me.

When I finished relating my experiences, I said, "Now all of you who want to know Jesus, I'd like you to come to the front of the church. And all of you young friends of mine who want to give your life to Jesus and have Him work out His perfect plan for your life, come." And my, I was thrilled as I saw those people come!

But when I saw that big man at the back step out into the aisle, and when my **father** knelt at the altar at the front of the church, I thought my heart would explode! I took my Bible and I experienced the greatest thrill of my life—to point my own dad to Jesus Christ.

And friends, all of this happened in the first twenty years of my life! In subsequent years I've experienced God's loving plan in many, **many** ways. And I can tell you: it really pays to surrender unconditionally to Jesus Christ.

I know His file has a beautiful blueprint for **you**!

*Rev. Jimmie Bersche is a National Evangelist of the Christian and Missionary Alliance. He served many years in a pastoral ministry in Pontiac, Michigan.*

# The Flask that Wouldn't Break

by Dr. Richard H. Harvey

THREE LECTURE PERIODS before the Thanksgiving holiday our chemistry professor always lectured against prayer. Every year his sarcastic ridicule had the kids in stitches.

At the end of each year he would say, "By the way, is there anybody here who still believes in prayer? Before I ask you to stand or raise your hand, let me tell you what I am going to do."

He would step in front of his lecture table. He'd turn around, pick up a glass flask, and hold the flask several feet over the classroom's concrete floor.

Then he would say: "Now, if there's anybody here who believes in prayer, I'm going to ask you to stand and pray that when I drop this flask it won't break. I want you to know, students, that all of your prayers and the prayers of your parents, and those of your Sunday School teachers, and those of your pastors (and I'm willing for you to bring them all here to pray for you)—all of these prayers combined can't keep that flask from breaking when I let it go!''

He'd been doing this, unchallenged, for 15 years. Talk about Goliath!

When I was a senior there came to the school a certain freshman. The upperclassmen always told new students what Dr. Lee would do. When some of them told this particular freshman about Dr. Lee, he asked, ''By the way, is there anybody in this school who still believes in prayer?''

''Well, we think there's one fellow who still believes in it,'' they answered. ''His name's Dick Harvey. He lives on North Main. We don't know the number.'' But they described my house.

One day there was a knock at my door. I opened it and there stood this freshman. ''Are you Dick Harvey?'' he said.

''Yes,'' I answered.

''Do you believe in prayer?''

''Yes.''

''Some of the upperclassmen told me that you were the only fellow in this school who believes in prayer.'' he stated. ''Can I come in?''

''Certainly,'' I said.

He continued: ''I want you to understand that I'm a born-again Christian. I'm majoring in chemistry—which is perhaps a foolish thing for me to do since I understand what Dr. Lee does. But God has shown me that He wants me to stand up to Dr. Lee.''

''I want you to pray that God will give me courage when Dr. Lee makes his challenge, and I also want you to pray that when he drops the flask, it won't break. I would appreciate it if every time you pray you would ask God about this, even when you say grace at the table. I've only got a couple of weeks

20

before Dr. Lee will make the challenge, and I want God to give me courage to stand up to him."

"All right," I said, "I'll pray with you."

Then he said, "Christ has given me the promise that if two shall agree as touching anything they shall ask, it **shall**—not maybe—it **shall** be done for them of the Father which is in heaven."

Well, I was majoring in chemistry because I intended to go to medical school following my college work, and I was downstairs in the qualitative analysis laboratory when the appointed hour came. About the time I knew Dr. Lee would defy prayer I went upstairs and stood in the back of the auditorium. My heart was full of fear. I was actually shaking. If you had been near me, you would have thought I had palsy!

Finally he came to the moment. He stepped in front of his desk and said, "Now, is there anyone here who still believes in prayer?" The freshman was seated near the middle of that big auditorium. There were about 300 students in the class. It was the largest single class in the college.

He rose to his feet, stepped into the aisle, and said, "Dr. Lee, I do."

"My, isn't this interesting?" said Dr. Lee. "We've got a fellow here who believes that God can answer prayer!" Then he turned to the challenger and said very sarcastically, "Do you believe that God will answer your prayer?"

"Yes, Dr. Lee," replied the freshman. "I'm sure that God will answer my prayer."

"Well," said Dr. Lee, "this is most interesting, isn't it? Maybe I'd better explain again what I am going to do."

So he went through the whole procedure: how he

would hold up the flask, open his hand, and let it drop. The flask would break into hundreds of pieces, he said, and there wasn't any power on earth or in heaven that would stop it from breaking.

After he had finished his speech he turned to the young man and said, "Do you still want to pray?" The freshman replied, "Yes, Dr. Lee, I do." "Well, isn't this interesting?" repeated Dr. Lee. "Now we'll all be real reverent while this young man prays." Oh, so sarcastic he was! And again he asked the freshman, "Are you ready?"

"Dr. Lee," said the freshman, "I have been ready for a long time."

"All right," said Dr. Lee, you go ahead and pray. We'll all bow our heads."

The young freshman didn't even bow his head. He just lifted his eyes toward heaven and said, "Dear Heavenly Father, in the name of Jesus, I thank You that You have heard me. For Your honour, and for Christ's name, and for the honour of Your servant who puts his trust in You, don't let this flask break. Amen."

Dr. Lee took the flask, held it out, opened his hand, and let it drop. And as the flask fell, God changed its course. He drew it in. Instead of falling straight to the floor, it hit the toe of Dr. Lee's shoe and rolled over.

**And it didn't break!**

The class gave Dr. Lee the hee-haw, and for the rest of the time he remained at the school, he never again lectured on prayer. God ended that once and for all.

You know, I went home and got down beside my bed and cried. I said, "Oh God, why didn't I stand up for You? Why didn't I have the courage to honor

Your name?"

They that put their trust in the Lord shall never be ashamed. The world is looking today for evidence that we have a living God, that He isn't dead, and that He answers the prayers of His people.

Perhaps the willingness I have had through the years to run risks for Christ's sake really goes back to the time when that young man stood alone and prayed that God would honor His name in that chemistry class.

To this day, though it happened many years ago, the story of the flask that wouldn't break is told on the campus of that school.

*Dr. Richard Harvey is one of the founders of Youth For Christ International. He has also served as a pastor, District Superintendent, and evangelist within his own denomination. This material, though given verbally, is also an excerpt from Dr. Harvey's book,* Seventy Years of Miracles, *1976, Horizon House Publishers, Beaverlodge, Alberta, Canada.*

## Marked Men

by Rev. K. Neill Foster

AS WE'VE BEEN LISTENING to the discussion about the body of the Lord Jesus, I have been thinking anew about my place in the kingdom of God. Maybe you have too. Maybe you have been wondering just what place is yours in God's kingdom. One thing I know: we all have our place. We all have a special role to play.

As I look at my own life and I see how the Lord has directed me in the ministry of summer camps, I wonder, "Where did this spring from? Why has God put me in a ministry of camps?"

I think part of the answer may be traced to my boyhood. When I was eight years old I went to a Bible Camp in Alberta's Peace River country. There I was confronted with the Gospel and converted to Jesus Christ. That was step one in my Bible Camp experiences. And what a crucial step it was!

A number of years later I was invited to minister at

a children's camp at Nakamun Point, Alberta. Arriving at the site, I was immediately impressed by its beauty. And almost simultaneously I began to think, "There's an opportunity here!"

The following year I directed my first Family Camp at Nakamun. I have been doing it every summer now for thirteen years.

As I look back, I now realize that our Family Camps are operating on a biblical principle. It's the principle of sanctification. To "sanctify" means "to set apart." When people separate themselves from the newspaper, the television, the home, the job, and the school—when they separate themselves from all of these to spend time with God and His Word and His people, they involve themselves in a spiritual act.

God thought this "setting apart" was so important for Israel that on three occasions each year the Old Testament Jews had a sort of camp meeting. Three times each year they separated from their usual activities to spend time in God's Word. If not in number, at least in nature, we follow that example here at Family Camp.

As I've thought about camp, I have realized that it is often in a camp-meeting atmosphere that God does something very important and wonderful: He marks men. Some of the most profound things God ever does in people's lives, He does in camp meetings. Why? Because at camp, people are set apart and open to the cumulative effect of God's powerful Word.

At Bible Camps people encounter God. And when people encounter God, they are irreversibly altered. They are marked by the Lord.

Abraham was marked by God. There came a time in

25

Abraham's life when he heard the voice of God so surely that he was willing to leave his family and friends to go to a foreign land. Later on, when he heard the voice again, he was willing to sacrifice his only son rather than disobey. These actions were not the actions of an ordinary man; they were the actions of a man whom God had marked.

Moses met God on a mountain. Forty days he spent with just God and himself at Camp Sinai. When he descended from the mountain, he descended with God's Law and a face that shone. Moses had been marked.

The patriarchs had similar experiences. Take Isaac. He was just a youth, maybe sixteen years old, when Abraham bound him to the altar and prepared to plunge a knife into him. Lying there on the altar, I believe Isaac was one very anxious youth!

And then God stepped in with that dramatic, last-second reprieve. I can't believe Isaac ever forgot that moment. It was a miracle, and I believe it marked Isaac ever after.

Jacob, too, had his encounter with God. It happened as he was returning to face the brother whose birthright he had swindled. Jacob was scared. He tried to sleep; he wound up wrestling. Maybe he wrestled with the Son of God. I really don't know.

But I know Jacob met God through that experience. In the morning, his name was not Jacob, the deceiver, but Israel, a prince with God. The Lord had left His mark.

Look in the prophets and you'll find the same thing. Crisis moments. Encounters with God. Isaiah said, "In the year that King Uzziah died I saw the Lord...." Have you ever seen the Lord? Have you ever had an encounter with God from which you will never recuperate? Have you ever been marked?

Jeremiah said, "The Lord put forth His hand and touched me." Have you ever felt God's hand? Have you ever known what is to have the hand of the Lord heavy upon you? It happens.

Ezekiel said, "I saw visions of God." Have you ever seen a vision? Some people have seen visions. Visions happen today.

What is a vision? I believe a vision is God's act of pulling back the curtain that separates this world from the world beyond. A vision occurs when God allows a person to see what he's not accustomed to seeing. A vision is an act of God which allows a person to see farther than he's ever seen before.

Do you know that everything that is real was first a vision? A chair, a car, a book. First they were visualized. Then they became realities. It is that way with absolutely everything.

And when God shows someone a vision, that person is marked. Marked by God. The reality that develops in their lives flows from the vision received.

You can go from the patriarchs to the prophets to the apostles. What about Peter? Peter, who had denied Jesus three times. Peter, who was afraid to say, "Lord, I love you," because he had denied his Lord. Peter, who could only say, "Lord, I like you"? (The word Peter uses in John Chapter 21 is a very weak word for love, similar to our "like.")

Peter was changed. Peter waited ten days in an upper room. And "when the day of Pentecost was fully come" Peter was marked. Marked for eternity by the Spirit of God. And it happened in an atmosphere remarkably like camp: a period of days, and then a blessing poured out.

Paul was the same. God had been working in his

27

life. He had shown him how Stephen faced death. Then finally there was that dramatic encounter on the road to Damascus. Paul was thrown to the ground. Blinded. Made speechless. Spoken to by Jesus Christ. How's that for something spectacular?

But the important thing was not the spiritual phenomena. The important thing was the spiritual work of change. For that day God marked Paul for all eternity.

Well, I've given you a kind of review so that I could make some observations. First, it takes God. It takes God to mark a man. Never try to manufacture God's mark. The true mark of God must come from God.

Second, it takes time. The disciples were in the upper room for ten days. We're in too big a hurry. It takes time to meet God. We sing, "Take time to be holy"—but we never take it. Isn't that true? We need to take time.

Third, there is often a specific day for the mark of God. For the apostles, it was the day of Pentecost. Ten days they waited—then, on that specific day, God marked them.

I've noticed it at camp, too. Often there is one specific day that is special. At this camp, it was Friday. Friday night. That was the peak.

I believe that if a man has spiritual discernment he can sense God's peak. And having sensed that God has sent His peak, he will not try to manufacture another one. There's a time. There's a place. We do well to recognize it.

Fourth, when God marks a man it takes all eternity for the results to unfold. God's marks are permanent. If you would ask me what I desire from God for myself, I would answer, "To have a heart that is covered—scarred if you will—with the marks of God."

I'd like to tell you a few personal experiences, and then I'm going to close. I have mentioned my conversion at age eight. That was God's initial mark.

The second mark came when I was twenty. It came through an old Pennsylvania preacher named Roland M. Gray. Mr. Gray rolled into conservative western Canada with an emphasis on healing and the Holy Spirit. "Be filled with the Spirit!" he preached.

One night that man's preaching really got to me. And to a number of others. There was brokenness. And plenty of tears. I went to the altar to be filled with the Holy Spirit. And nothing happened.

The next night brother Gray preached again. There was not that brokenness. There was not that emotion. And not one person went to the altar.

I was leaving the meeting when brother Gray spotted me and asked, "Neill, why didn't you come back and pray?" And by "pray" he meant, "pray until you're filled with the Holy Spirit and know it." (You see, he knew that had not yet happened to me.)

Well, he had asked me a question, and I had to respond. "I didn't feel like it," I said.

"You come back whether you feel like it or not and God will meet you."

I looked at his gray hair and decided he should know what he was talking about. The following night I came back. I had them place their hands on me. I said, "Lord, I'm going to believe that you have filled me with the Holy Spirit."

I stood up. I didn't feel a thing. But I knew that the Spirit of God had come upon me. I was marked by God.

Some of you were over at Nakamun when Brother

Terranova preached there. Some of you remember him preaching about Abraham and the altar of love. As he spoke, I had to stand beside him and interpret his Spanish.

One part I didn't want to interpret. It was when he said, "Now you must love your brother. Turn to that person beside you and say, 'I love you.' "

If you were there, you remember it. We were hesitant at first. But then something broke. Maybe in part it was our Anglo-Saxon reserve giving way to Latin persuasiveness. But far more, it was the power of the Spirit of God. Because suddenly that whole camp-meeting tabernacle was washed in God's love.

And again I was marked. God had gotten to the reluctant interpreter, and for the first time I can remember, I said to my parents that day, "I love you, Mom. I love you, Dad."

I have since carried that message of love to Africa. In the town of Dedougou, Zaire I preached a message on "observable love." Love that you can see, and feel, and hear. At the end of that message, I said to my interpreter (and former pastor), Jerry McGarvey, "I love you, brother." He replied, "I love you, too."

Then the two of us went down among the Africans. In their African language, we said to them, "I love you. I love you."

Over at one side of the church a missionary reached out in love to an African. The two broke down together in tears.

And then it happened. Love exploded! Africans went to Africans, blacks went to whites, whites went to blacks. And all of them were saying the same beautiful words: "I love you! I love you!"

I saw a big missionary—over six feet, maybe close

to 250 pounds—bawling like a baby. I saw a little African houseboy—a new Christian believer—with tears pouring down his black face. What did they have in common? They had been marked. Marked by love and by God. And I know they will never again be quite the same.

Some Africans from Dedougou went with me to Bono. I said, "Lord, can it happen twice?" And the Lord gave me the Scripture, "The voice of the Lord is upon many waters." I took it to mean, "God doesn't always do this, but He can do it again."

We had hardly begun in Bono when the missionaries there began making wrong things right. I hadn't told them to do it. They did it on their own.

That was the tone at Bono. People getting right with God. People getting right with other people. The meetings went on for four or five days, with a long meeting in the morning and another long meeting at night. On the last day, we met from 9:30 in the morning until 6:30 at night.

What were we doing all that time? Confessing our sins. Making things right. Those Africans would get up and make things right and then they'd break down and cry. And then we'd pray for them.

Finally, after four days, everything had been settled among all the missionaries and African preachers present? I said, "Have we all come to the place where we can raise our hands (their custom to show that they are at peace with one another) and be at peace?"

"Yes!" They all raised their hands. We were all at peace.

I proceeded to preach a very short message on Pentecost. When I had finished we prayed together and said, "Oh God, fill us with the Holy Spirit."

You know what happened? We actually **heard** the Spirit of God come upon us. Or maybe it was simply our corporate human reaction to the Spirit's coming. I don't know.

You say, "Did He manifest Himself?" Yes, he did. How did He do it? By another explosion of love. Abundant love and abundant tears.

All I'll say is this: I'll never recover from that day. Never ever! I was marked. Marked by God. There has to be a God to mark us. It takes time. But when God puts His mark on you, He changes you. Praise God, He changes you. Hallelujah!

Now listen. Most of us know each other well. You want God to mark you. Are you open? Do you need to be saved? Get saved. Do you need to be filled with the Holy Spirit? Believe God—He'll do it. Do you need to be healed? Let God heal you. He'll do it.

You say, "I'm walking with God. I'm saved. I've been filled with the Holy Spirit. But I know there's more." Of course there is. For as long as you live, there's more.

Why is there more? Because God is still in the business of marking people. He's still at work: altering people's lives, changing their lives, intervening miraculously and supernaturally for good. That's why I really believe in camp meetings!

*Rev. K. Neill Foster is the author of three books, editor of the Canadian Christian tabloid* Communicate *and an evangelist. He also was the Director of the summer conventions where the material contained in this book was delivered.*

# Rotten Egged

by Dr. Glen V. Tingley, Sr.

THE ROTTEN-EGG story began when I was twenty-seven. That was many years ago, and it was then that I accepted a task: to establish a church in a city where our denomination had no churches—Birmingham, Alabama.

I began by becoming the pastor of our nearest work, a 23-member fellowship in a Birmingham suburb. After many very unusual experiences, we moved out of the suburb and into the city.

We opened in a downtown theatre. Before long, we erected downtown a big, board, tabernacle-tent.

And then the sparks began to fly. That downtown tabernacle-tent was to become the focus of a war that was the most wonderful, delightful thing that ever happened to me!

First, the Ministerial Association tried to persuade me to tear the structure down. They offered to pay

33

all the expenses of a radio program I had and to make me evangelist for the association if I would do so. But the tabernacle was not to be moved and neither was I. I refused the preachers' offer.

Our real struggle, however, came not with the ministers, but with the incumbents of City Hall. One day the city firemen came and put a padlock on the tabernacle door. I was out of town preaching at the time, and when I found out what had happened I rushed home and called my attorney. I told him to meet me at the mayor's office.

When we got there, the mayor said, "The tabernacle must come down." I turned to my attorney and said, "Judge, you go and get an injunction against them. I'm going to get a gun and blow that lock off the door!" "You can't do it!" said the mayor. I said, "You watch me do it. Come on down, I'll show you how it's done!"

When I got down to the tabernacle brandishing the firearm, the firemen were there removing the lock. Righteous indignation had apparently paid off!

Every week after that the mayor sent me a paper saying that I would tear down our building by a specified date. I was supposed to sign the paper and send it back. I went half way: each week I sent the unsigned paper back!

A newspaper reporter learned of the ongoing commotion and decided to look into it. After getting both sides of the dispute, he wrote an article. The next day a big, bold headline splashed the controversy across the paper's front page!

A number of weeks later I went back to see the mayor. I had discovered that the Salvation Army, the Volunteers of America, Howard College, and the Wesleyan Methodists all had a permit to preach on

34

the street. Figuring I should have one too, I told the mayor, "I want a permit to preach on the street!"

"I'm not going to give you a permit," replied the mayor. I protested, "But Howard College has one, the Salvation Army has one, and all those others have one. You can't discriminate." He replied, "I'm going to discriminate against you! You can't have one."

"Well, I'm going to preach on the street anyway," I said. "I'll arrest you," he warned. I replied, "That will be good. I have always wanted to be jailed for preaching the Gospel. This is a perfect opportunity!" I walked out with the mayor flinging new invectives at me.

A newspaper reporter was outside the mayor's office and overheard our conversation. He talked to the mayor when I left; he later talked to me. The following day another Tingley-City Hall dispute made the news!

I wisely put off preaching on the street for a week or more. But when I did take to the street, did I have a crowd! The spectators filled an entire block! There were not tens, nor hundreds, but thousands of people there!

City Hall sent down five policemen to arrest me—but not one of them laid a hand on me. A year later I learned why. An organization in Birmingham had fifty men on hand with instructions that if any of those five policemen touched me, they were to hoist all five of them on to their shoulders, march down to City Hall with them, and dump them in the mayor's office! So I didn't get to be arrested for preaching the Gospel after all!

After a few weeks of street meetings the crowds slackened and I prayed, "Lord, should I stop these? What should I do?"

35

Then one day some very bold girls from the "red-light district" drove by our meeting in a car and let loose with a barrage of eggs. They were aiming at me, of course, but they hit Lawrence Greenway, my assistant.

It was wonderful! It was a marvellous story for the headlines: "**Tingley Rotten Egged on the Street.**" I contacted the newspapers and when they printed the story my crowds picked up!

One time we had such a throng of people downtown that traffic had to be diverted for blocks. They called out two squads of policemen. They called out the fire apparatus from three fire stations. They planned to break up that crowd and to do it they were going to douse the crowd with water.

But when they got out the hose, some of the men on the scene said, "If you turn that hose on the crowd we'll take it away and turn it on you!" The firemen didn't want to get wet—they kept the hose turned off!

In the midst of all the furor I booked the 22,000-seat Legion Stadium for a Sunday-night rally to proclaim what was wrong with the city administration. I was going to clean house!

We advertised that rally on big signs at our street meetings. At one of those meetings, a girl who had been converted out of the redlight district was holding a sign advertising the rally when suddenly once again the eggs began to fly!

One of the eggs hit the girl's sign, splashing down over top of her. Pulling the egg from her eye, she said, "Praise the Lord—throw another one!" Smash! Right down over her again. Disgustedly, she cleaned the egg off again, and said, "Praise the Lord," but not, "Throw more!"

It came time for the Birmingham city election. To my delight, the incumbent gang was voted out, though they had been in office for many years. Some of my best friends were voted in, men who gave me every courtesy. Then, when the county election came up, the incumbents were also voted out and my best friends were elected. As far as I know, I haven't had an enemy in office since—and that was thirty-nine years ago.

In the government shakeup a very dear friend of mine was elected county sheriff. Although the city officials had been voted out, in actuality they were still holding power, and my sheriff friend said to me, "I wish we could do something about that Buster Jackson gang."

"What about them?" I asked. He said, "They operate in Chicago, Birmingham, and Miami and they're flooding Birmingham with bootleg liquor. They aren't operating in the county—if they were, I'd get them. They're only in the city and they're paying protection.

"I'm afraid we can't get them until the change in administration. And even then I'm afraid they'll have the police force tied up for a long time with hush money." I began to pray and I prayed right then with my sheriff friend, "Lord, help us to get the Buster Jackson gang."

One day I was speaking over the radio and I said, "Today at the Lyric Theatre there is going to be a noonday service. We invite you all to come." As I said those words a local nurse was sleeping off a drunken orgy with the Buster Jackson gang.

As that nurse turned over in bed her toe flipped the switch on the radio at the foot of her bed. She woke up hearing me invite people to come and worship at the Lyric Theatre. She thought it was a voice from heaven!

She got up and dressed as in a trance, and came down to the theatre that noon. She was among those who came forward and were converted to Christ that day.

Sometime later she said to me, "I'd like to tell you my story." Then she proceeded to tell me how wicked she had been. When she told me she'd been with the Buster Jackson gang, my ears pricked up and I asked, "Do you know Buster Jackson?"

"Yes," she replied. I said, "Can you buy me some liquor from him?" She answered, "Yes, if he hasn't heard that I've gotten religion." I said, "All right. I want you to buy a fifth of whiskey from him."

She went over to a telephone booth where the call couldn't be traced, and she called Buster Jackson. And she managed to buy me a bottle of bootlegged whiskey.

Can you imagine the consternation in the city when I purchased a quarter of a page in the newspaper to say: **"I will show you a fifth of whiskey that I purchased from the Buster Jackson gang, the gang the city of Birmingham says it can't catch. I will tell you how you can purchase one."**

I tell you we had a time. We were in a tent and when it was time for the service you couldn't get near that tent. Two dear old ladies who had been converted and who had previously seen something of the rough, seamy-side of life said to me, "Brother Tingley, don't you dare go behind that pulpit. Buster Jackson's gang will kill you."

"I'm going in there," I said. "I'd love to be killed for Jesus!"

I preached that night and gave a gospel invitation

for people to give their lives to Christ. A young tough who had been sitting on the second seat (and who had a 275-pound usher keeping vigil behind him) came forward to pray. At the altar he said to me, "I've got a confession to make. I was sent here by the Buster Jackson gang to shoot you."

He reached into his shirt and pulled out a gun. He laid it on the altar and wept. "I want to know Jesus Christ as my Saviour, and I couldn't be right without confessing this to you," he said. The last time I heard of that man, he was operating a Christian Mission, more than twenty years later.

"That I might gain them that are without the law, who have no knowledge of righteousness at all. That I might gain the weak...." There are a lot of weak folks in this world. I have an incident that will illustrate it.

I was on my way to a barber shop one day when I met a newspaper boy yelling, "Paper! Paper! Read all about it! '**Tingley Rotten Egged Again**!' " I bought a paper because that story interested me!

I was still reading the account as I walked slowly into the barber shop. The barber had a paper, too, and as I got into his chair I said, "Boy, it looks like they are about to get that preacher, doesn't it?" He said, "Yes, sir. And I'd like to be in the gang that gets him!"

As he shaved me I learned that he wanted to tar and feather me. He thought up different things he'd like to do, and whenever conversation lagged a little I just egged him on a bit more. I said to him, "What's the matter with the fool?" "Oh," he said, "he's always asking for money." I said, "Probably the fool doesn't know how to get it without asking for it!"

When he had finished shaving me, I paid him and stuck out my hand and said, "What's your name?"

He gave me his name. I looked him in the eye and said, "My name's Tingley." Have you ever seen a man turn every color of the rainbow at the same time? He did!

I went out of the shop and got into my car. He followed me out to the car muttering, "I-I-I don't know whether I should apologize or not." I said, "No—I think it's very funny. I appreciate a joke, especially when it's on myself."

Then I asked him, "Are you a Christian?" "Well, I'm a church member," he answered. I said, "Church members go to hell, they need Jesus Christ. God wants to save you and I'm surely going to pray for you."

I went back about a week later and that barber had gone out of business and closed up shop. Four years later he told an assistant of mine what had happened. He said, "I had to close up shop and go to work in Nashville, Tennessee. I drove 250 miles every weekend in order to keep away from him lest he'd get hold of me and I'd become as crazy about religion as he is!"

I was on my way to Jasper, Alabama one time when a police officer stopped me for speeding. "Where's the fire?" he asked. I said, "In Jasper." He asked me what I meant. I said, "Jasper's on fire and going to hell and I'm on my way to see if I can rescue some people!"

"You must be Tingley!" said the officer. I said, "I am." And all he said was, "Get on!"

Preachers, don't be afraid to attempt big things. Attempt the ridiculous things, and then people will come out to see what a fool you are and they'll make up the crowd!

One year I rented that 22,000-seat Legion Stadium

40

for every Sunday night during the month of August. **The Birmingham News** said that there were 10,000 people out every Sunday night to hear the local preacher. Hundreds were converted. One of them was the policeman who stopped me on my way to the "fire" in Jasper!

Friend, let me tell you something. The grace of Jesus Christ can touch anybody, anybody at all, and change him. It can make a new creature out of any mortal. There isn't a person in the world who cannot find a solution in Jesus Christ if he'll give Him a chance.

Let me make one more application. I've seen a multitude of fine Christians, but they were as powerless as could be and as empty as last year's bird's nest. They didn't have anything to shout about, they grumbled a lot, and yet they claimed to be Christians. They thought that holiness was associated with a long face. That notion is a curse to Christianity!

Have you ever wondered what "more than conqueror" means? We find a classic illustration of it in the New Testament. The apostle Paul turned trouble into triumph. When a deranged girl followed Paul and Silas screaming, "These men are servants of the most high God!" Paul let her draw a crowd and then he preached Jesus!

I wouldn't have amounted to anything if it hadn't been for my enemies. God bless those dear, wonderful people who sought to do me evil. They made me! People came out to hear me preach who wouldn't have paid the slightest attention if I had been a calm, doleful little preacher who never stood up to anyone. They came out to see what kind of a critter I was!

41

Listen—God wants us to do exploits for Him. Most of us preachers just draw our breath and draw our salary, and not much of either. It's a pitiable situation. We're afraid to stir people. We're afraid to stand up for what's right or to ever oppose anybody.

One of the things that happened in Birmingham was that Christians suddenly caught fire. They began to tell others about Christ. And for more than half of those first seventeen years if you came to my church late you were more likely to stand than sit. The place was that full!

Christian friend, mark this, you and I ought to be able to speak with authority to anybody about Jesus Christ. We expect our missionaries overseas to go to every hut and share Jesus Christ. But what about us? I've said to many preachers, "Have you visited every home in this town?" "Well, no, I haven't," they say. And I say, "What have you been doing? That's the first thing you ought to do."

Many a time I've made more than forty calls a day ringing doorbells and saying, "I'm Glen Tingley, pastor down at the tabernacle. I'm going to preach on Sunday night on such and such a subject." It packed the church and many found Christ and then told others.

No wonder in those early days we had more than 2,000 people accept Jesus Christ as Lord and Saviour every year. One year we had 6,000 confess Jesus Christ. Today (1967—ed.) in Greater Birmingham our denomination has fifteen churches.

The church I started and pastored grew to 1,400 members and God is still blessing its ministry. I say that not boastfully, the Lord knows, but I tell you, you've got to do something with people! I sent them to other denominations, but our churches started anyway.

All I'm saying is this: "That by all means I might save some." We need a revival of fervor, a revival of passion, a revival that goes from door to door, from heart to heart, from lost soul to lost soul, from neglectful soul to neglectful soul—until everybody in an area has heard about Jesus.

Jesus Christ wants us to do something!

*Dr. Glen V. Tingley is a pastor of the Christian and Missionary Alliance. He has also served as a National Evangelist in North America and overseas.*

# The Widow-Maker Missed Me

by Rev. Delbert McKenzie

WHEN I RETURNED home that dull October evening the first words my wife, Jane, said were: "I knew you were in danger today. After you left me this morning I could do nothing but pray for you."

Later that evening one of the men in the church came over to cut up an elk I had shot while hunting the week before. As we got into the car to go down the street to get it out of a friend's garage he said, "Del, what happened to you up there today? About nine or nine-thirty this morning I just had the deepest feeling that you were in danger. I even had to stop my painting and find a room where I could be alone and pray for you."

The next day I went to Coeur D'Alene, Idaho, to a seminar for Alliance pastors. On the way I stopped at Plummer, Idaho, to see Rev. and Mrs. Gene Clott. Mrs. Clott answered the doorbell and when I stepped in she said, "We've just been talking about you!''

When I asked why, Gene replied, "Yesterday morning about nine or nine-thirty we were praying together when we suddenly felt that you were somehow in danger. We don't often pray for you, but we felt that we had to protect you by prayer. The burden lasted for about fifteen minutes and then we knew you were safe.''

What had brought about this miracle of God moving upon the hearts of four people in different places, some of them separated by more than eighty miles, and all of them more than fifty miles from me?

One of the men in our church, Ursel McPherson, was working on a slashing job in the mountains north of Lewiston. Because he needed help and because I had been a logger before entering the ministry, I often went up on Mondays to run a chain saw for him.

That particular morning I left about five o'clock. When I arrived where he was working quite a strong wind was blowing. We decided to fell trees anyway.

Shortly after nine o'clock I cut a tree which the wind blew into another one. Foolishly, I left it leaning and went on to another tree. Later I walked under it and, forgetting that the widow-maker was still there, cut the tree it was leaning against. Just as I pulled the chain saw from the one I was felling, I saw a blurr of the descending tree out of the corner of my eye and lurched backward.

When I regained consciousness sometime later I realized that the tree had hit me on the head. The inside of my mouth felt like hamburger. Almost all my teeth were loose. Blood ran down my face.

I shut off the saw, which was lying between my feet and still running. I found my glasses on the ground.

45

When I put them on and tried to walk I discovered my equilibrium was gone. I half walked and half dragged myself from stump to tree to stump to tree until I reached the road.

Ursel was working on his chain saw at the truck and came to meet me. After he got me down on some coats by the truck we prayed. Several minutes later I felt well enough to get up. When I did, I found my balance had been regained.

Then an awful fear gripped me. I had never known such fear of death before, even though I had had many close calls while working. I talked to God about it and He indicated that I should go back to the saw and start again.

Shortly afterward my eyesight became blurred again. I would walk up to a tree and see two or three. I asked God to restore my eyesight. Instantly it was normal.

A few minutes later severe pain developed in the back of my head. Again I turned to God. This time it took several minutes of earnest prayer as I worked. Soon, however, the headache was gone.

I worked the rest of that day and returned home in the evening. Everything healed properly. My teeth tightened. The only evidence left today is one tooth which settled in crooked. My wife wanted me to see a doctor just to be sure I was all right, but God had already done so much that it seemed like a waste of time and money!

There have been absolutely no later effects, and that was nearly two years ago! Praise God for His protection even when we are careless.

The following Sunday I shared this experience with the people of our church. We were thrilled as we saw how the Holy Spirit had moved on the hearts of people many miles apart. If they had not prayed, and if God had not allowed me to see that tree just in time to lurch away, I would have been instantly killed. Had the tree hit two inches to the left it would have been squarely on the top of the hard hat. The force would have broken me to pieces.

The Spirit of God has used that experience to lead our church as a body of believers into a greater ministry of intercession. We have learned to love and care for each other in a much greater way.

As great as the experience was, however, I robbed God of the glory which He alone is worthy to receive. When I would tell the story I would imply that it was just a freak accident. I did not admit that I had been foolish enough to leave a tree leaning and then walk under it.

I have since confessed my sin of deceit to the people who were told the experience. The evening it was confessed to the people of our church God's spirit moved in on us and we have had a gracious and wonderful moving of His Spirit since.

Our hearts are filled with adoration and praise to our God who so cares for us and is so forgiving when we turn from our self and sin to seek Him!

*Rev. Delbert McKenzie is a pastor and conference speaker. Currently he ministers in Lewiston, Idaho. Though his material is reprinted by permission from* The Alliance Witness, *it was also given verbally in the 1975 Saskatchewan convention.*

# The Shepherd's Psalm

## by Rev. Bill Weston

THE SUNDAY SCHOOL teacher had just completed her lesson on the twenty-third psalm when one of her students, a nine-year-old boy, declared, "I don't think it means that." Incensed, the teacher reprimanded the boy and told him he ought to respect his elders. To that, the little fellow announced, "Okay. When I get big, I'll find out for myself."

When that nine-year-old troublemaker grew up, he became the president of a large university. He had money, power, prestige. He also had an unresolved desire: to discover the full meaning behind the Bible's psalms. He longed to travel to Israel to see the shepherds in action for himself. So he took a leave of absence from his post and set out to fulfill this lifelong wish.

Upon returning from Israel, the university

president shared his observations. So doing, he had a marvellous ministry of shedding light on the psalms, including the twenty-third psalm. And today as we consider this "shepherd's psalm," I'd like to include some of this man's fascinating observations regarding sheep and shepherds.

The psalm begins, "**The Lord is my Shepherd**." God compares us to sheep. There's a good reason for that. Of all the members of God's animal kingdom, sheep are perhaps the most likely to get lost. You take a dog or a cat, and you have an animal with an ability to navigate that is sometimes astonishing. I once heard about a dog who found his way from Arizona to his old home porch in New Hampshire! A sheep could never do that. Once a sheep becomes disoriented, he's lost. He will not find his way home; someone must go look for him.

We are like sheep; we need a Shepherd. David said, "The Lord is **my** Shepherd." It was a personal thing. Is He **your** Shepherd? He wants to be. Do you know Him personally? You can if you want!

"**I shall not want**" is self explanatory. Philippians 4:19 is still in the Book: "My God shall supply all your needs according to His riches in glory by Christ Jesus." If you're a Christian, God has promised to provide for every single need. Why? Because the Shepherd takes care of His sheep.

"**He maketh me to lie down in green pastures**." The university president noticed that after the sheep had grazed for awhile, the shepherds would make them lie down. Like some people, some of the sheep didn't want to lie down. "Why do you make the sheep lie down?" he asked. "Why don't you let them continue to graze?"

"Well, sir," said the shepherd, "I get paid to

produce fat, slick, healthy sheep. And sir, whether a sheep becomes fat, healthy and sleek does not depend on how much the sheep eats. It depends on how much the sheep assimilates.

"You see, sheep are cud-chewing animals. After they have grazed, they must lie down and chew their cuds. As they chew their cuds, they put on fat, which produces oil and a better fleece. So we make them lie down—if they ran around eating all the time, they could get lean just because they didn't pause to assimiliate."

And brother, do we have that in Christendom today! We've got sermon tasters. A lot of church tramps who run around grabbing a bite at one church, taking a nibble at another church, and so on. And what these people so often really need is to sit down and assimiliate—to take time to allow their spiritual food to properly digest and become part of their lives.

Some of you are just too busy. Some of you, God love you, have such a tight schedule that if you missed the first section of a revolving door on Monday morning your whole week would be upset!

But hear it, beloved, if you're too busy for God, you're just too busy. And God might have to make you lie down so that He can talk to you. It takes time to be holy! If you won't take the time yourself, God might have to help you take time. He might even have to put you on the flat of your back in a hospital. Don't make him do that—decide for yourself to "take time to be holy...to spend much time in secret with Jesus alone." Believe me, it'll do you good!

"**He leadeth me beside the still waters.**" As the university president watched the shepherds, he frequently saw them get down on their knees beside a rushing stream and pull the rock and mud over to the side of the current. He could see that they were forming quiet little pools for the sheep to drink from. Intrigued, he wondered why.

One day he asked a shepherd, "Why don't the sheep drink directly from the stream like any other animal?"

The shepherd looked at him and said, "You don't know very much about sheep, do you? Sir, probably more than any other animal, sheep do not like to drink from disquieted waters. Knowing this, we build quiet little pools where they can drink in peace as the stream rushes by in front of them. And when the walls of the little drinking pools erode we rebuild them."

As the president related this, he said, "You know, beloved, if you'd just watch, you'd find that in the midst of your busy schedules the Good Shepherd has prepared for you quiet little pools of spiritual refreshment. If you neglect to drink from these pools, you will not be equipped to face the spiritual tests that come your way."

He was right. All of us are blessed with quiet little pools, times when we can pause briefly and be spiritually refreshed. You say, "Not me! I'm too busy!" Oh? How about all that time for leisure, for entertainment? Mom, how about that time you spend watching "The Edge of Night"? Dad, how about when you're driving to work? All of us have times when we can talk to God or read a few lines from His Word. And often we can pray or meditate on a portion of God's Word as we go about our daily activities. Practice this—you'll find God's quiet little pools very refreshing!

**"He restoreth my soul. He leadeth me in the paths**

51

**of righteousness for His name's sake**." The university president said that often as the sheep were grazing, one of them would suddenly raise its head and bound over to the shepherd. There, it would rub its head against the shepherd's legs, and the shepherd would get down on his knees and gather the sheep into his arms. The shepherd would scratch the sheep's ears, fondle it, and then pat it on the back and send it back to the flock. And then another sheep would come to receive the same treatment.

One day the president asked a shepherd, "Hey, what's happening?"

"Why do the sheep come, sir?" said the shepherd. "The only reason I know is that they just want to be loved."

Listen, beloved. When did you last come into the presence of God just to be loved? When did you last come into God's presence and say, "Lord, you know what? I'm delighted with You. I don't need a single thing. I'm just here to tell You I love You!"

Try it some time. And after you've expressed your love to God, just be quiet and let Him love you back. It's tremendous!

Well, one day the president saw a sheep that just refused to be loved. The shepherd would try to pick up that sheep and it would back away and stomp its foot. It did not want to be loved.

Intrigued by this sheep's abnormal behaviour, the university president mentioned the stubborn sheep to the shepherd. "Just wait, sir," said the shepherd coldly. "We shepherds know how to restore our sheep. Just wait!"

The president waited for several days. During that time, he saw the shepherd try desperately to win that sheep through love. He watched as the shepherd tried to entice the sheep by offering it choice morsels of food. And he saw the sheep crane its neck to get the food, and then withdraw its neck to get away! It wanted the shepherd's food, but it did not want the shepherd's love!

One day the shepherd walked by the president and said very simply, "Today." And that day the president watched as the shepherd tried for nearly two hours to reach that stubborn, scared sheep through love. And he could see that once again it just wasn't working.

As the president continued to watch that stubborn sheep, he suddenly realized that the shepherd had changed his position and was now turned slightly sideways. He had one arm behind his back; he was concealing something from the sheep.

The sheep ate his goodies and was just about to bound away, when suddenly from behind the shepherd's back flashed his rod. He struck that sheep with a lightning blow that sent it sprawling in the dust. And then he threw the rod away and gathered that sheep into his arms and caressed it and fondled it for about two hours.

When the shepherd finally set the sheep down again, it didn't want to leave. The shepherd had conquered. The rod had achieved what love alone could not achieve.

Beloved, I've had the rod used on me. It has never been fun. It has always hurt. Please son, listen daughter, don't force God to use the rod on you. Don't say, "Butt out, God!" He loves you—but if you won't respond to His love, He'll come with His corrective rod.

I have an uncle in Pennsylvania who told me a true story about a young man and a young woman in his church. The young man was the Sunday School superintendent; the young woman was the church pianist. It was a natural—they fell in love and got married.

God blessed that union with a flaxen-haired little girl named Mary Jane. Everybody loved that cute little tyke. She was delightful!

But as Mary Jane got a little older, she got spoiled. By the time she was five or six, she had become a regular little brat! One Sunday morning, little Mary Jane threw a temper tantrum. John, her daddy, said, "Honey, she just doesn't want to go to Sunday School."

His wife, however, wasn't so sure. She said, "Darling, I don't know why she's upset. You get a substitute to play for me and I'll try to find out what's the matter. Mary Jane and I will miss Sunday School and come along later for church."

The next Sunday, that little rascal put on the same act—same time, same station. And her parents reacted the same way—Mom again stayed home with Mary Jane.

When the following Sunday it happened for the third time, John wasn't going to be put off. "Honey, that's temper," he said. "I'm going to lay it to her. She's got to learn."

"Don't you dare, John!" responded his wife. "Don't you dare lay a hand on my child." And John didn't. Instead, he once again went off to Sunday School alone.

John's wife stopped attending Sunday School and church altogether. And John followed her. What was happening? They were giving in to every whim of little Mary Jane. And they were leaving God right out of their lives.

Well, what happened? One day like a bolt out of the blue, God reached down into a home in Pennsylvania and removed a flaxen-haired girl of seven. With very little warning, Mary Jane took sick and died.

My uncle said that at the funeral John sobbed uncontrollably. His young wife, however, didn't shed a tear. Her lips were drawn into a thin line and the beauty was gone from her face. She was mad at God. God had taken Mary Jane.

As time passed, that young woman remained bitter. One day as John returned from work, she met him at the door and poured out her hostility: "I hate this place!" she said. "Everything in it reminds me of Mary Jane. And I have to stay in it all day while you go off to your business. If you loved me, John, you'd get me out of here."

"Honey, wait a minute!" John retorted. "I loved that girl just as much as you did. You're just not facing life. You've made a shrine out of her room. You've ceased to act like a wife. And if you don't quit acting like this, I've had it. Our marriage has had it!" And he turned on his heel and went back to his place of business.

Before long, he returned to say, "Come on, we're leaving."

"What do you mean? What are you talking about?"

"You wanted to get out of here and now we're leaving. I've made plans for an extended trip—we'll be gone for about three months."

So they left the country and went travelling throughout Europe and beyond. But everywhere they went, their troubles went with them. They could not escape.

Finally, they arrived in the Holy Land. And it was there, as they watched an Eastern shepherd and his sheep, that finally God was able to break through to that young woman's hardened heart.

Sitting on a Judean hillside, the young couple watched one day as a shepherd led his flock of sheep to the edge of a stream of rushing, knee-deep water. The shepherd forded the stream, expecting his sheep to follow. The sheep refused. The shepherd pleaded with those sheep, but still they would not cross the stream.

Finally, in desperation, the shepherd waded back through the stream to where his disobedient sheep were rolling in the grass. He bent down, picked up a little lamb, and carried it across the stream to the other side.

Separated from its mother by a stream of rushing water, the unhappy little sheep began to bleat. The mother sheep walked up to the stream's edge, looked at the tumbling, frightening water, and plunged in. And the whole flock followed her over to the other side.

As that bitter young woman watched this from the hillside, God got to her. She grasped her husband's hand and sobbed. She said, "John, did you see what I just saw? That shepherd took that little sheep across the stream to the other side. That's what God did with our little lamb, Mary Jane. He took her over to the other side.

"And just like that bleating little lamb, honey, can't you hear **our** little lamb calling, 'Mom, Daddy, come this way?' It reminds me, John, of that Scripture verse we learned in Sunday School. The one that says, 'Where your treasure is, there will your heart be also.'

"John, God took our treasure to the other side. I couldn't rear her properly. I gave in to her every little whim. I'd have spoiled her completely.

"And honey, we've cut God out of everything. It was my fault. I led the way, darling. Please forgive me."

By then, that young woman was in her husband's arms. God had gotten through, and in an unexpected way their trip had paid off. They were ready to return home.

My uncle told me about the Sunday morning that couple returned to their church. The minister was speaking when the door opened and in they came. They walked right to the front of the church. When the minister realized what was happening, he came down from the pulpit and met them. "What is it, John?" he asked. "Is there something I can do?"

John replied, "Sir, we had to go thousands of miles to learn a very bitter lesson: God didn't forsake us; we forsook God. He had to use a rod on us, sir, taking our little one out of our home.

"And sir, we have come directly from the airport. We didn't mean to interrupt things like this, but we just got back and we couldn't wait to be restored. Would you pray for us?"

And there in that church that young couple met God. Christ was restored to their hearts and lives. The lesson had been hard, but at last they had learned it.

**"Yea, though I walk through the valley of the shadow of death, I will fear no evil. Thy rod and thy staff, they comfort me."** The university president said that one day while he was with a shepherd, the shepherd called his attention to a rock face that extended upward for almost three hundred and fifty feet.

"Up there, sir," said the shepherd, "is one of the

finest grazing lands in this part of the country. Do you notice that little path leading up there? Well, sir, you and I could walk up that path in relative safety. But as for the lambs, I'm not so sure. One of them might fall and kill itself. And sir, if any shepherd loses three sheep in a season, he won't be hired the following season. So we take no chances."

And so rather than risk a little lamb, that shepherd led his flock two and one-half miles to get to a place that was just three hundred and fifty feet away if he had taken the trail. But when he finally arrived, he had all of his sheep. Not one had been lost.

Do you know what? Look at me, Dad. I've heard dads say to me so many times, "Hey, Bill, I can do this. It doesn't hurt my conscience any." But how about that little guy who's watching you, Dad? He thinks you're the greatest thing that ever breathed. Can he follow in your footsteps? Would you feel comfortable if he did?

"**Thou preparest a table before me in the presence of mine enemies**." Beloved, this is the verse that the university president questioned when he was a boy of nine. And many years later the Judean shepherds helped him to finally understand its meaning.

He noticed that before the shepherds would turn the sheep loose in certain pastures, each would take from his cloak or pouch a trawl-like instrument with which he would dig up a certain kind of weed. Wherever these weeds appeared, the shepherd would dig them up and bury them.

Before the sheep were allowed to enter the pasture, the shepherds would do something else. They'd go over to where there were little mounds of earth with silver-dollar-sized holes, and they would pour liquid down those holes. As the president watched, he

58

could see fumes rising from the outpoured liquid.

He was intrigued by these two matters, and so one day he asked, "What is the weed, sir, that you're digging up and burying and what is the liquid that you're pouring down the holes?"

"Well, sir," the shepherd answered, "the weed is poisonous. The sheep aren't likely to eat it because of its odor. But if they do happen to eat it, it could make them very sick. So we just dig it up and bury it."

"And the holes, sir?"

"Little snakes live in those holes. They'll lie there with their heads protruding just above the surface, where they can bite our sheep in the legs. And the snakes are really far more dangerous than the poisonous weeds. The weeds can make the sheep sick; the snake bites can kill them.

"And so that's why we pour the liquid down the snakes' holes. The fumes of the liquid kill the snakes. And once the snakes are dead, the sheep can graze in safety."

Beloved, why were those sheep able to graze in safety? Because the shepherd had gone before them and taken the sting out of death. Does that say anything to you tonight? Listen, son, daughter. Hear it, Mom and Dad. Jesus Christ is the Good Shepherd. He died for you. He took the sting out of death so that you could follow where He leads. He wants to meet all your needs. He wants to lead you to pastures of plenty. Will you follow him?

"**Surely goodness and mercy shall follow me all the days of my life and I shall dwell in the house of the Lord forever**." The university president said that every evening those Judean shepherds would watch their sheep as they returned to the fold. If one of the sheep had been injured during the day, the shepherd would call that one aside and minister to its needs. He'd pour oil on its wound and bandage it. And only then would he allow the wounded sheep to join the others in the fold.

When the sheep were finally resting at the day's conclusion, the shepherd would wrap his great cloak around his body and lie down. Where? In the entrance to the sheepfold. He'd lie between the sleeping sheep and any outside danger.

That's what God is like. He's the supreme Protector. He stations Himself between His sheep and any invading danger. And unlike the Judean shepherd, He neither slumbers nor sleeps.

How about you tonight? Do you know Jesus as your own personal Shepherd? Can you say from your heart, "The Lord is **my** Shepherd?" If you can't, won't you come to Him? He offers eternal, abundant life. And he offers it now—to you.

*Rev. Bill Weston is the long-time Director of St. Louis Youth for Christ. He also travelled for a number of years as song leader for his beloved father, W.G. "Daddy" Weston.*

# Kiss the Doorknob!

by Rev. Nathan Penland

OUR TOPIC is the spiritual inheritance of the Christian. As Christians we are thinking about who we are, what we are, and what we have in Christ Jesus. And we are talking about becoming what we are meant to be—mature Christians.

You know, it is a wholesome thing to long to grow. It is good to want to be mature. Certainly if there would be anything that would grieve my heart it would be for one of my children not to have grown properly or developed physically. It is a wholesome thing to want to grow and develop physically.

It is also a wholesome thing to want to grow and develop spiritually. One burden and deep prayer of my heart has been, "Oh God, don't let me get so busy saving a world that I let my own flesh and blood, my own children, go to hell. Let me so live among them and so discipline and love them that they will want to know the Christ their father knows." And to God be the glory, and I say this with all sincerity and humbleness of heart, all of our five children have come to know Him at an early age.

I've heard my wife say to our boys, "Now boys, eat some of that spinach." And I've heard my boys say, "Uggh, yuk! A hog wouldn't eat this!"

I've noticed that many parents do the same thing. They plan and coerce and manipulate to get their children to eat what they should. Why? Because they know a proper diet is essential to proper, healthy growth.

But when it comes to spiritual growth, many of these same parents reverse the rule. Instead of making certain their children get a proper spiritual diet, they leave their children to themselves.

Such parents say to me, "Brother Penland, we don't make our children always sit up in church and listen because they don't understand anyway and we're afraid that if we force them they'll get bitter." They say, "We don't have devotions at home regularly because if we force our kids to listen to the Bible too much they might come to hate God."

Why is it that we take a positive approach to the physical and a negative approach to the spiritual? The Old Testament Jews were instructed to write the scriptures on their doorposts and to talk about the scriptures on the streets and in the markets. They lived with the Book! Moms and dads, never fear going to church regularly and having regular family devotions.

My parents always took their children to church and we always sat in what was known as "Penland pew." I sat with my parents until I was about 15. Then my dad said to me, "Now, son, you can sit anywhere you want, but you had better not sit in the back of the church, and you had better not sit with a bunch of boys who will be whispering or laughing. The first time I catch you making noise you'll come right back up to our family pew—I don't care if you're a hundred years old!''

My parents weren't wealthy, but they gave me a rich spiritual heritage. I had to work my way through six years of Bible school, but I had a marvellous time doing it!

The first Christmas I came home from Bible school my father and mother apologized for not being able to pay my way. I said, ''Dad, don't you ever say that again! You have given me a love for the Lord and His Word, and through your life and influence you have brought me to Christ and you have given me the miracle of physical life and good care. When you are dead and gone these things will remain.'' I thank God for the inheritance I have from my parents.

But I also thank God for the spiritual inheritance I have from Jesus Christ. This inheritance includes all the wonderful privileges of membership in God's family. It is a glorious gift from a wonderful Giver!

What is my response to such a Giver? I am instructed, through Paul, to ''walk worthy of the Lord....'' How is your walk this morning as a child of God? Someone has said, ''I don't care how loud you talk, but I want to know how you walk.''

Our walk ought to back up our talk. What we say ought to reflect what we are.

I am reminded of a story about ''Dad'' Weston and a football game. Dad Weston was a great and beloved preacher. This story involves his son, Bill.

At the time, Bill was a high school football player. His team had made it to the finals and Bill and his teammates faced an all-important game. If they didn't win, it was elimination. Bill asked his dad to come and cheer.

The game was almost over when Bill got the ball and scored a touchdown. In the excitement of the moment, Dad Weston jumped to his feet and hollered, "Hallelujah! Praise God! Hallelujah!"

"But Dad," said his wife, "this is a football game!"

"I don't care," said Dad. "What's in must come out and that's what's in!"

Sometimes, however, what comes out of a man in the pinch isn't his Christianity. Some people seem to think that Christianity is a Sunday thing. They shave up and fix up and groom up and put on their best suit. But when they get home from church and shut the door, the cats and dogs have to scurry for shelter! (Someone has said that when a fellow gets soundly converted and filled with the Holy Spirit, the cats and the dogs always know it!)

Many of us want people to think we are more "holy" or "spiritual" than we really are. Probably all of us at times are a bit fictitious, and there is something about us that still has the taint and smell of earth. And there are times, I know in my own heart, when I am ashamed of myself.

I remember one time when I arrived home from my church late at night. I was a tired pastor who hadn't finished half his day's work. I fell into bed, seeking sleep.

After a rather restless night, I got up early the next morning. I was edgy. I wanted to get going. I wanted to get down to the church and get the other pastors and the secretaries going.

That morning my wife had some things for me to

do. I did some of them, took the ki
came back to the house. I was hurr
church office on time and to myself
she keeps this up, I'm going to

On my way out the door my wife s
is garbage day. Would you please
out of the basement? They just ha

I swelled up like a toad frog and
see fire coming out my ears. I
basement and came back with on
arm, had to go back down for the
pull the garage door, and all the
into the house to wash my hands
"Kiss me goodbye."

"Kiss the doorknob!" I exploded
all alike, you have no mercy on a
end to it." I slammed the door (n
I said, "Have a good day and

I roared off in my car. And at th
my Bible out and the big Rev. Pe
church downtown gathered t
workers and read the Bible. It
Sears-Roebuck catalogue. It di
There was no God around any

That over, the phone rang. I
mixed-up people wanting help
mixed up than she was. Finally
and you call back tomorrow." I
and said I would be gone for

I went home and knocked on th
opened it and said, "Honey,
back?"

"You know what I'm doing
ashamed of the way I acted.
called a husband, nor a father

gra
a pa
coul
wan
The
so o
agai
It's
The
and
Go
that
But
says,
heav
a frui
life is
live i
arou
My
"Lor
Let th
Yours
Wall
gentl
am co
will c
we ha
That
and p
judge
fruit a
accou
One
we dr

ddad, but most of all I'm not worthy to be called
stor by hundreds of people who look up to me. I
dn't get my work done. God has left me and I
t you to forgive me.''

n my wife said, "Oh, honey, it was me." And
n. And I said, "Honey, let's not start all over
n. Let's stop it here!"

none of your business what we did then!

Lord was with us and I went back to the office
had as good a day as I've had in all my life.
l wants us to have a spiritual walk. I thank God
He can live with us day by day.

Paul not only says, "Walk worthy." He also
"Be fruitful." This is not talking about
en—this is for now. God wants each of us to live
tful life. The Christian's inheritance now in this
a worthy, fruitful walk. Paul said, "For me to
s Christ." We are to be little Christs walking
d. Christ wants to live through us.

prayer just before coming to this meeting was,
l, let me be Jesus in this pulpit this morning.
ese lips be Yours. Father, hide me, but show
elf.''

k worthy, being fruitful. And ladies and
men, it is the Holy Spirit who produces fruit. I
nvinced that at the judgment time the reward
me for those times when in yielded obedience
ve allowed the Holy Spirit to work through us.
which we have done in the energy and ability
ersonality of the human flesh alone will be
l worthless. It is the Holy Spirit who produces
nd every Christian will one day have to give
t for the fruit of his life.

f the things I said to my wife and my son as
ove to this camp was, "Let's not be like

sponges which absorb everything and have to be crushed to give out. That's tragic. Let us ask God to give us fruit on these grounds.''

Brothers and sisters, let us walk worthy of the Lord, being fruitful, increasing in the knowledge of God, strengthened by God's power. This is God's glorious plan for all of us.

*Rev. Nathan Penland was formerly a pastor in Asheville, North Carolina. He now serves as an evangelist, both overseas and in North America.*

# Visions Precede Reality

by Rev. Carmelo Terranova

WE LIVE in a very interesting epoch. We're at an historical vortex, where the various factors of the past converge and the great happenings of the future are being prepared. There has never been an age like this one. This is the hour of the restoration of all things—the prophetic word, the revelation of the kingdom of God, and the vision of the glory of God.

The days are coming when these revelations of the future will all be realities. In Acts chapter two, Peter twice declares, "...these are the last days." When did the last days begin? At Pentecost. They began at Pentecost, but they are culminating now. We are living in the last of the last days!

The prophet Ezekiel points to this time in history. His book contains a great dream, a moving vision, and a prophetic tenderness. It demonstrates the crucial relationship between a vision and reality.

Everything that is real was first a vision. First a thing is visualized, or dreamed—then it becomes a reality. Before the reality of Ezekiel's ministry, there came to him a vision and a dream. Without great dreams, it is impossible to have great realities.

A great enterprise was first the dream of a founder. A great marriage was first the dream of a man and a woman. A great church was first the dream of a pastor. Every great reality was first a great dream.

The man who never dreams never does anything great. It is the great dreamers of history who have changed the world, philosophically, politically, culturally.

It is the same way spiritually. And in the spiritual realm, the greatest dreamer of all is God Himself. God's dream is the Church. The Church was God's dream before the world ever existed. Before man was ever created, the universal, glorious Church of Jesus Christ existed in the heart of God, a great, passionate dream of the Father from the beginning of time.

God's dream is expressed in the Bible. It is insinuated in the lives of the Israeli patriarchs, it is narrated in the Bible's historical books, it is poetically sung in The Book of Psalms, it is desperately anticipated in The Song of Solomon, and it is further revealed in the life of Jesus, the lives of his followers, and in the revelation given to the apostle John.

The Church. God's dream. It is the great vision of the future, recorded by John in The Revelation. One day the completed Church will be a reality.

But though we cannot yet see the completed Church, we can feel God's passion for the Church, His dream. And through faith in Jesus Christ, we can be a part of the Church!

Why does God give people great visions, great dreams? Not to thrill them, but to show them reality. And then to lead them into that reality. Every great vision is the precursor of a great work. God gives visions to build His Church!

Tragically, many visions don't build anything. Many people see a vision, but never see their vision realized.

Listen. God sends His visions for a purpose. Every God-sent vision is intended to produce action. And every action that comes from a vision of God promotes God's cause.

What is the tragedy of the contemporary church? It has lost the vision of its eternal destiny. The Bible says, "...where there is no vision, the people perish." People perish when they fail to see the vision, the prophetic revelation, the unfolding of the Church of Jesus Christ.

God prepared Ezekiel for his future work by giving him a great vision, a vision that completely changed his life. Many people today can relate to Ezekiel's vision.

We think we live in difficult times. We read of the biblical saints. and we say, "Today it is different. Today, it is much more difficult to live for God." That is not true. It was as difficult then as it is today.

It was difficult for Abraham in his day. The Bible says that he was one man, alone, just one, in the corrupted days of the city of Ur, when paganism had arrived at one of its most abject levels. That was difficult! But Abraham had a secret resource—the vision of the call of God to a distant land. And Abraham embraced that vision. Just one man, alone, but with God and a vision, it was enough.

Moses was alone in Egypt. But he, too, had a vision of the call of God. He heard God's voice, saw the burning bush, and went to the top of the holy mountain. He had the forces of Egypt against him. Among his own people he had a million critics, including his own brother. But Moses became one of the meekest, strongest men of history. What did he have? A vision of God. He could see ahead to God's distant triumph.

For Paul, life was also difficult. And, to be sure, life is difficult now. But it is not the difficulty of the circumstances that counts. We are what counts.

Ezekiel had a great work ahead of him, and God had to equip him for that work. He lived in a time of depression and shame, a miserable, captive Jew. But God was preparing him for a great ministry. Part of that preparation was a great vision.

We read about Ezekiel's vision in Ezekiel chapter one. It is a vision of the likeness of the glory of Jehovah. When I read it I fall on my face and listen for the voice of God.

What is a vision? Is it something strange, something mysterious? The word "vision" is very interesting. It is made up of two parts, which together mean to see beyond what the eyes can see, to see beyond the normal eyesight. There is a limit to what we can normally see. A vision goes beyond that limit.

A few years ago I was taking a course at the university in Asuncion, Paraguay, when a very famous eye surgeon came to lecture to our class. One of his statements grabbed my attention. He said that the human eye is capable of seeing 100,000 times more than it does. If a certain protective covering were removed, he said, the eye could see 100,000 times more than it does now.

In a spiritual sense, a vision is God's act of removing that covering. A vision is God's act of allowing us to see what we couldn't see before. It is illustrated by an incident from the life of Elisha.

One day Elisha's servant came to him with the news that the enemy Syrians had surrounded their city. "Don't worry!" said Elisha calmly. "Those who are with us are more than those who are with them."

Then Elisha prayed, asking God to open the eyes of his foolish, frightened servant. And God removed the covering from that servant's eyes, enabling him to see what he had never seen before—horses and chariots of fire of the Lord of hosts covering the mountainside, surrounding Elisha.

Beloved, we need a vision like that. We need to know that those who are with us are more than those who are against us. We need to know that we are surrounded by the armies of God. We're not alone. God's world surrounds us, and if we could only see, without limitation, we would see the hosts of God surrounding us and protecting us. We can't see them, but they are there.

But there is another aspect to a vision. Sometimes God gives visions to enable a person to see what no one else sees. Ezekiel saw what no one else saw—the vision of the glory of God.

The Christian Church needs to recover that vision—the vision of the glory of God. When we understand God's glory, our lives will change, we will discover God's unlimited power, and God's irresistible love will surround us. A clear vision of God will change our way of living.

I have discovered that there are two types of

churches—those that have the triumphant, glorious vision of God, and those that have absolutely no vision of God's glory. I see this clearly in the campaigns I conduct as I travel to churches throughout the world.

In one type of church I see a great deal happening—lots of prayer, lots of promotion. People are expecting great things. They live intensely. They say, "Wonderful things are going to happen. We'll have miracles. God will do great things." They pray in their homes and they pray in their church. They wait for great things and they receive great things. The results are the product of their great vision.

But there is also the other type of church. In it, the people say, "A preacher is coming. Let's see what he's like and what he can do!" And then they sit down to listen. They don't hope for anything, and nothing happens.

It all depends on the vision. The practical objective of every vision is to focus us on God, to make us able to see Him.

What did Ezekiel see? In chapter one, verse four, he declares, "And I looked, and behold, a whirlwind came out of the north, a great cloud, and a fire infolding itself, and a brightness was about it, and out of the midst thereof as the colour of amber, out of the midst of the fire." This is a very impressive verse. There are three things that we will see in it.

First, it is a revelation of God the Father—the wind of His power, the cloud of His glory, the fire of His holiness, the radiance of His presence.

It is a glimpse of what God the Father really is. I like to read the prophets. What a vision of God they had! They saw God as great and powerful, the God of their fathers, the God of the nations, the God of the armies, the sovereign God, the God who fills the world and the universe, the great God! They had a great God and they were great men.

What makes a man's life great? The kind of God he has! You are not small—your god is small! You are not great—your God is great! The measure of your greatness is your vision of God. There aren't great men, there aren't little men; there are men with a vision of a great God, and men without any vision of God at all. Ezekiel was a man with a vision of the great Father God.

But there is more. There is also a picture of Christ here. The four portraits of Christ (the accounts of Matthew, Mark, Luke, and John) are synthesized in Ezekiel chapter one, verse ten: "As for the likeness of their faces, they four had the face of a man, and the face of a lion, on the right side: and they four had the face of an ox on the left side; they four also had the face of an eagle."

Here we have Christ pictured as the Son of Man (the man), the King of Kings (the lion), the tireless Servant (the ox), and the Son of God (the eagle that soars through the distant heavens).

How Ezekiel's vision of Christ moves my heart! On the one side He is the Son of Man; on the other side He is the Son of God.

Jesus is the Son of Man. What is man? Where is a representative man? Where is the authentic man, the prototype of humanity? Where is the example of what man should be? Where is such a man? Christ is the Man, the great Man, the Giant of history, the Product of historical dreams. Blessed be the Lord Jesus Christ! Glory to His name! He's the Son of Man.

But He is the Son of God too. What is God like?

How does He feel? How does He dream? God is like Christ, His Son. Jesus is the reflection of God's glory, the splendour of His holiness, the fire of His power, the wind of heaven. Hallelujah!

Jesus is the Son of God. And Ezekiel saw this vision of Christ and fell in love with Him. He's the Son of Man, the King of Kings, the Lord of lords, the tireless Servant, and the Son of God.

I have this vision of God. Do you have it? It can change your life!

But there's more. In verse twelve we read, "And they went every one straight forward: whither the spirit was to go, they went; and they turned not when they went." Here we have the Holy Spirit, the One who moves and guides. We find Him moving in harmonious unity with the Father and the Son.

On the captive frontier of Babylon, the unknown, unheralded Ezekiel had a blessed vision of the great triune God—Father, Son, and Holy Spirit. Ezekiel saw and he believed and his life was changed!

Ezekiel looked at God, saw His power, saw His tenderness, and saw His love. That vision changed his life. That vision changed history. God wants such a vision of Himself in **your** life!

If there is no vision, there is no life; if there are no dreams, there are no realities, no greatness, no glory, nothing. How's your vision?

*Rev. Carmelo Terranova is an Argentine evangelist and international Bible teacher. He was formerly Vice-President of the Alianza, Cristiana y Misionera of Argentina.*

# The Love Message

by Rev. Duane Morscheck

BACK IN 1971 at the Family Camp at Nakamun Point, I heard a message by Carmelo Terranova on the topic of love. It was a message that really changed my life, perhaps more than any other message I have ever heard.

Today I feel it would be honoring to God for me to share from my life and to speak on the topic of God's love. Frankly, I'm not sure that without Brother Terranova's message I could honestly say what I'm going to say to you now: "I love you. I love you in the Lord."

You say, "You don't know me! That doesn't make any difference. You say, "You don't know what I've done!" That doesn't make any difference either.

You see, God has shown me that loving is a **responsibility**. It is not something you do only when you feel like it or when you feel "moved." It is not something you do only when you see some special problem or need in a life. Loving is something you do "straight across the board." Why? Because loving is a commandment of the Lord.

I find that every time I preach this message, God makes new to me some special thought from His Word. And the thought that really quickens in my heart this morning is found in I John 4:7,8: "Beloved, let us love one another: for love is of God; and every one that loveth is born of God, and knoweth God. He that loveth not knoweth not God; for God is love."

Oh, my! "He that loveth not knoweth not God; for God is love." God is the very expression of love. Jesus Christ was God's love placed into the world in the flesh. Jesus was love in action.

God has made me realize that I really have to love **everybody**. Not just my family and my friends—but everybody. Even the unlovely. Even those who hate in return. Everybody!

You say, "What kind of love is this?" I'll tell you what kind of love it is—it's God's love. God's love shed abroad in our hearts by the Holy Spirit who is given to us. And my friend, if you want to know the reality of obedience to God in the area of loving, you need to be filled with God's Spirit so that love can operate. If you want a new dimension to your love, if you want a love that won't quit, a love that suffers long and stays kind, a love that reaches beyond the endurance of human mind and human strength and human heart—then you need the love of God shed abroad in your heart.

The apostle Paul had this supernatural love shed

abroad in **his** heart. In I Thessalonians 3:12, he wrote: "And the Lord make you to increase and abound in love one toward another...." And even as everybody said, "Amen," he added, "and toward **all men**." Again, it's everybody that we must love!

You know, you can have a lot, but if you don't have love, it's really nothing. You can do a lot—and yet, without love, it's nothing. You can have abilities that dazzle people—but without love, those abilities are like clanging gongs and tinkling cymbals. We must have love—toward each other and toward all men.

Some people think that love is soft. It isn't. That rugged man of God called the apostle Paul closed a letter by saying, "My love be with you all in Jesus Christ." Think of it! Paul was saying, "I just love each one of you!"

Oh, there are so many illustrations I could give! I've seen love change peoples' lives! When nothing else can get to a person, love can! Friend, you learn to love, and you're far down the road to pleasing God.

And one thing you'll find, friend, is this: When you find this love, and begin to express it, and begin to live it, you're going to need a bigger basket. Because God will keep pouring His love back into you. And there will be love streaming toward you through people, too. It'll be wonderful!

But what's the purpose of love? In I Thessalonians 3:13, Paul tells us: "To the end that He may establish your hearts unblameable in holiness before God." Friend, holiness and love go hand in hand. Any "holiness" that doesn't love is counterfeit.

You know what I've found? I've found that what we

need in our lives today is to come to the place where we love—not just in deed and in truth—but also in word and in tongue. We can err in either direction. I believe we need to verbally express our love.

As I left Nakamun in 1971, I was determined to express God's love, in God's way, for God's glory.

One day, God laid it on my heart to express this love to a close friend who worked in a garage as a mechanic. So I walked up to him in the garage when he was alone, and I said, "Irv, have I told you lately that I love you in the Lord?"

A smile as big as all outdoors broke over Irv's face. And believe it or not—that simple act changed Irv's life. I don't believe anything quite like it had ever happened to him before. Oh, what it does to a human being to feel the warm, fresh, clean, pure love of God coming to him from another person! It makes a difference.

You say, "It wouldn't make any difference to me!" Well, just try it! It **will** make a difference. Yes, even to you!

I remember how God dealt with me. I used to find it hard to love people I couldn't help. I had no problem loving people I could help. I had problems with the ones I **couldn't** help.

One time after I had spoken rather critically to a husband and wife, that wife came to me and said, "Brother Morscheck, you don't really love my husband and me in the Lord, do you?"

You know, those words were the hardest I'd ever heard. I don't hurt easily. But those words really got to me. And the only answer I could give that dear lady in that hour was this: "I can't answer that question the way I'd like to, but I want to answer it right."

After a few moments she left. And then I cried. Like Hezekiah and David, I "cried unto the Lord." I really bawled. I said, "God, I've got to have freedom from this."

And then God showed me my problem—a censorious spirit that just wouldn't quit. He showed me how that spirit of fault-finding had manifested itself and hurt people at different times and places throughout my life. He made my problem very clear.

But then He set me free. Oh, I'm thankful for that! And that evening before the service began, I met with that husband and wife and God enabled me to say to them from the depths of my heart, "I love you in the Lord."

Who do you suppose came to the altar for help that night? That man and his wife! And because faith worked by love, God revealed to me their problem and I was able to help them. Praise God!

As I began showing God's love to people, God showed me that I had never expressed my love to my stepfather. So He gave me a good opportunity to do it—He arranged for me to return to my old home town for a week-long series of meetings. And while there, I stayed with my mother and stepfather.

I know it sounds strange—but I tried all week to say to my dad those simple words of love. All week long I tried to express to my stepdad that I loved him in the Lord, and the words just wouldn't come.

Oh, it was hard! Finally, just as I was about to leave for the airport, I said it: "Dad, I want to tell you I love you."

How could three words mean so much? Those words changed our whole relationship! My stepdad had been good to me, provided well for me, encouraged me in many ways. But before I said those words, "I love you," there had never been a free flow of love. And when I finally did say those words, something good happened to both of us. Friends, God wants His love to **flow**!

Brother Terranova showed us **so** much about love. I remember how that summer as he ended his message, he said, "We're going to express our love this morning. First of all, we're going to express our love to God."

And as he led us that day, we all said, "I love You, Lord." It's amazing how many times we sing it—how many times do we just say it? We **need** to say it! Let's do it now!

After we had expressed our love to God, Brother Terranova said, "Now we need to express our love to each other." And he had us turn to the person seated beside us and do it.

That's what I desire for you today. I want you to know what it is to turn to that person beside you and simply say, "I love you in the Lord."

You say, "I don't feel it!" No matter! Loving is an act of the **will**. Expressing that love is also an act of the will.

And by deliberately doing these acts, we honor God and allow His love to flow. And when God's love flows freely, we discover for ourselves: "Love is the greatest!" It really is!

*Rev. Duane Morscheck is an evangelist and itinerant Bible teacher from Billings, Montana.*

# A Broken Home
## and
## a Broken Heart

by Nickie Stansberry

ONE NIGHT a number of years ago I had the privilege of singing at a meeting where a Dr. Feinberg of Talbot Theological Seminary was the speaker. After the meeting concluded, I was introduced to Dr. Feinberg, who said, "Mrs. Stansberry, I understand that you are a native of Wales?"

"Yes," I answered.

"You are Welsh?"

"Yes," I replied.

He turned to the pastor beside him. "I have great respect for the Welsh people," he said loudly. "They are the one people who thoroughly disprove the theory that men come from monkeys."

"What?" I thought.

Then he concluded, "Because the Welsh people come from whales!"

A lot of you have noticed that I have a slight accent, and have asked where I come from. My accent is

Welsh; originally I came from Wales!

The Welsh people, I think, are better known for their love for music than for anything else. In my own life, this love for music surfaced early. When I was only two or three years old, my mother would take me to town and, once there, sometimes lose me in the crowd. On my own, I would invariably gravitate to where music was playing. And my mother would find me by the music, with my skirt up, dancing. From the time I was very tiny, I loved to dance.

I was an "only-child" for many years and although my family was not rich, my mother's wish was that I would one day have a stage career. I shared her desire. I thought that to have a stage career would be the most wonderful thing in the world!

At the age of fifteen I became the soloist for a dance orchestra. Singing with the orchestra meant dropping out of Sunday School, but that didn't really bother me then. The God I worshipped was very remote. I had never heard anyone give a personal testimony concerning God. I had never been told that God was interested in me personally. I thought that God was to be consulted only in case of an emergency. Naturally, I didn't think to consult Him about whether He wanted me to drop out of Sunday School!

I was still fifteen when I got a chance to audition for the Harry Roy Orchestra—at that time probably the leading dance orchestra in Great Britain. Before the audition, I was interviewed by a man who told me that if I didn't have my own financial backing, I would have to "like men." "Do you like men?" he asked.

"Of course I do!" (What normal fifteen-year-old girl doesn't like men?)

And then the man was very kind to me and let me know that my stage career would certainly depend on my attitude toward men. He wanted me to understand that before I auditioned.

I went through with the audition and was told to see them in London. But I never went. I wanted no part of their way of living. And to this day I'm glad for that. I'm glad for my early moral training in Sunday School and at home.

I decided that what I really wanted in life was a happy marriage. And there's nothing wrong with that, except that once again I was making my plans without any thought of God. The thought that He could lead me to the right man for my life never even occured to me.

I was incurably romantic. I was in and out of love every week! My girlfriend and I would talk about our plans and we'd watch the married couples and the courting couples as they walked along the street. They were easy to distinguish: the courting couples would stroll along hand-in-hand gazing into each other's eyes; the married couples would walk about a mile apart never looking at one another!

And then, one day, the man of my dreams came along and I really fell in love. He was an American officer and he swept me off my feet completely. Oh, I'll tell you! He didn't say too much; he just acted. He gave me everything he thought I needed and more.

When we were married I was the envy of all my friends. I think if a poll had been taken at the time, our marriage would have been voted the marriage "most likely to succeed."

By the time my husband and I left Wales, we had a little baby. I idolized my husband and I eagerly anticipated moving to what I believed was the most wonderful country in the world—the United States of America. Leaving Wales, I was bursting with excitement!

We moved seven or eight times during our first year in the United States. We scuttled from place to place and from job to job. Times were tough—but I felt that as long as I had my husband I had everything. And I was totally and completely convinced of my husband's love for me.

About the time our second baby was born, everything seemed to cave in. Within a three-month period, it was one thing after another: Our new-born baby almost died of pneumonia and had to be hospitalized, the daddy lost his job because he had an emergency appendectomy, and we lost our house because it was part of my husband's job. As a result, the bills piled.

But those piling bills didn't seem to matter. I loved my husband and felt certain he loved me. For me it was enough.

But as I was expecting our third child, people tried to tell me that something was wrong. I wouldn't accept it; yet in time I knew it was true. I knew my husband was spending less and less time at home. And I could tell something was very wrong just by looking at his face.

Just before our third baby was born, the thing I thought impossible, the thing I thought could never happen to me, happened. My husband, confused and upset, left our home. And my heart, for the first time in my life, was crushed into a million pieces.

Many things happened—things too personal to share. Result—at twenty-two years of age, I felt that I was "all washed up." I couldn't cope. I decided I would walk down Highway 99 and throw myself in front of the first car that came along.

I went out to Highway 99 and I walked and I walked and I walked. But I just couldn't do it. I returned to the home where I was staying.

After the baby was born, the daddy returned and I was bolstered tremendously. I had told him, "If you change your mind, come back." And I want to say now, I'm glad. I'm glad I took him back. I know now that nothing he did was done to be cruel.

When my husband came back, we started life afresh. We didn't speak much about it, but I know that we both sensed the need for an extra dimension to our lives.

So we opened our home to a cult. Friends of my husband belonged to a cult and we agreed to let them use our home for Bible study. But a cult wasn't what we needed. We needed Christ. Oh, how we needed Jesus Christ! And to this day I ask those people, "Why didn't you tell us about Jesus?"

They didn't tell us about Jesus. They told us about their little theory of when you should worship and why their church was the only true church.

People, don't preach your church. Preach Jesus! Jesus said, "If I be lifted up, I'll draw all men to me." And I have never forgotten that.

One night at the Bible Study I mentioned something about Easter, and they said, "Oh, that's a pagan holiday!"

That touched off a big argument. My husband got so angry he said, "You can leave this home! Either stick to the Bible or leave!" They left.

We waited for their reaction. Would they still have us to dinner on Friday night? Would they still be our friends? No, they had nothing more to do with us.

When my husband saw their reaction, he said, "That's it! Religion is for somebody else—not me. They're nothing but a bunch of hypocrites!" And from then on, he had nothing more to do with religion. I longed for him to go to church with me. But he never would.

So I went alone at Easter and Christmas. Don't make fun of that! Don't criticize when someone goes to church only at Easter. There has to be some interest for a person to even do that. But even when I went to church at Easter, still I never heard the Gospel.

In our home, things continued to get worse. And again I won't go into details, but I'll tell you this much: life can become hell on earth. And marriage, I believe, was meant to be a little heaven on earth. And it can be—when God plans it and Christ is Head of the home. I really believe that!

But home, for me, was anything but heaven. I was totally unprepared for rearing a family. As a girl back in Wales, I had never even babysat! Before my first child, I had only once even seen a new-born baby. And in America, I found myself expecting child number five! I had to depend very heavily on the daddy for everything.

I can remember nights when I would walk the floor and cry out to God. I'd throw myself on the floor and wail, "Oh God—please help me!" But my prayers just bounced back at me. They didn't seem to go any farther than the ceiling.

Then one day a babysitter asked my children to come to Sunday School. I thought, "You know, I don't have any money to give the kids, but I can give them something spiritual." So I sent them off to Sunday School.

And sending the kids to Sunday School brought the pastor around. Thank God for pastors and laymen who visit! And thank God for the prayers that began to go up for my family and me.

But when those prayers began the devil really went to work. He "came in like a flood"—and things in my life got more confusing than ever!

Some Roman Catholic friends of my husband wanted to give us their literature. Some Mormons came to our door, and since my husband wasn't home, I invited them in. Soon they began holding weekly Bible studies in our home.

I liked the Mormons. I liked the answers they gave. They were very kind to me. And I was ready to become a Mormon, when God completely removed the Mormons from my life. Christians had prayed for me and I myself had prayed, "Who's right, God?" Removing the Mormons was part of His answer.

At the very same time, my husband again left the home, this time never to return. He left me with five children (I was expecting the sixth), and practically no money or resources to care for those children. Worse, he left me with the heartrending knowledge that I had been forsaken by the man I had trusted. And once again, just before Christmas, my world fell to pieces.

But you know, because of the love of God's people, it was the best Christmas we ever experienced. I can't tell you all the wonderful things those people did to show their love. And through them I was exposed to the gospel for the very first time.

You can imagine how much I needed God. And you're probably thinking, "Boy, she probably went forward the very first time she was invited to an altar!" I wish that were my testimony. But it isn't. It was to be two years before I gave my life to Christ.

People don't always understand the Gospel right away. I didn't. There was so much confusion in my life that when I heard people give personal religious "testimonies," I didn't understand what they were talking about. When I heard laymen praying or people crying, I couldn't understand what was going on. And when I heard the pastor weep and invite people to come to the altar, I felt like saying, "Pastor, that was a really good sermon. Don't cry!" And I would go home and pray for the pastor. After all, I liked him and he preached well, even though I couldn't understand him! I'd pray, too, that God would either help me to understand those people or get me out of there before I went crazy!

I did not feel comfortable in the church. When the people asked me if I was "saved," I said, "yes." I thought I was a Christian and I thought "Are you a Christian?" was the question they were really asking. So "yes" seemed like a proper answer.

I definitely didn't want fanaticism. I thought, "You go to the altar, cry a whole lot, then get up and give a testimony and they'll accept you as a Christian." And the devil told me, "You don't have to do that! You're just as good as they are. You believe that Jesus is God's Son. There's no need to make a spectacle of yourself!"

But I'll tell you something—those sermons on sin really bothered me. Listening to them, I'd get so uncomfortable I couldn't stand it. Oh, how I mentally defended myself: "I'm not a sinner. I'm a good mother. I'm a good neighbor. I try to do the best I can. And God's good. He'll take me to heaven. These people are fanatics. Oh, sure, I like them. Sure, they're good to me. But they're fanatics!" Oh, I was uncomfortable!

But God showed me, through the light of His Word, that I was a sinner. He showed me in a beautiful way through a sermon on judgment. But still I refused to go to the altar.

There were times during those two years when I really wanted to walk right out of those church services. "I don't belong here," I thought. "I've got to get out of here! I want to go where people dance. I want to go where people live. I don't want to die—I don't want to live like these people live. Lord, I want to really live. Please get me out of here!"

The people were not naturally attractive to me. They did not have bubbling, sparkling personalities. Their dress was drab. They didn't dance. They didn't do a lot of things that I found attractive.

But do you know what they did do? Those people loved me. Every need I had, they met. They took my children to parades. On Thanksgiving Day, when my family and I were all alone, one of the families shared their home with us. Those people did so many things that I will never, ever be able to repay. Through the people of that church, I felt the love of God. And that alone is what kept me attending until I

90

found Christ for myself.

Finally one night God showed me the real problem of my heart: pride. For two years I had been uncomfortable in that church. I had said I was a Christian. I had even given testimonies about God's love. But I had always resisted God's urging to go the altar. I had been too afraid of what people would think.

I had been leaning on the lie that all the people wanted was emotion. And God shattered that lie. How? He had the evangelist give an illustration that really got to me. And the one who had always hated emotion began to cry. And I didn't care who saw me cry. Because I knew that it was nothing but pride that had kept me from God.

I was the first one forward to the altar that night. All I remember was a consuming desire to rid myself of a heavy, heavy load of pride.

But when I got up from my knees, I discovered that I had received much more. For the first time ever, I understood the testimonies. I bubbled with joy. I wanted to say again and again, "It's real! Jesus Christ is real! I understand what you're talking about!"

God changed me that night. He showed me what the Scriptures mean and He made Jesus Christ very real to me. God can do a wonderful thing with a broken heart when He gets all the pieces!

And now, with the psalmist David, I can say, "It was good for me that I was afflicted, that I might learn thy statutes." And with the songwriter I can say, "He washed my eyes with tears that I might see."

In closing, I want to testify that I found reality in Jesus. I found truth—in Jesus. I found life—real life—in Jesus. In Jesus I found love that is eternal and unchanging.

I found One who said that He would be a Father to the fatherless and a Husband to the widow. I found One who said that He would meet our every need according to His riches in glory. And he has always done that. He has clothed us and fed us. He has satisfied my heart completely.

And one time when I was lonely and wanting a husband, He gave me these wonderful words from Isaiah:

> **"Fear not, ye will no longer live in shame. The shame of your youth and the sorrows of widowhood will be remembered no more.**
>
> **For your Creator will be your Husband. The Lord of Hosts is His name. He is your Redeemer, the Holy One of Israel, the God of all earth.**
>
> **For the Lord has called you back from your grief, a young wife abandoned by her husband.**
>
> **For a brief moment I abandoned you, but with great compassion I will gather you."**

Praise the Lord!

He gave me a chance to return to the British Isles, there to testify for Him through gospel music. He gave me the joy of seeing my mother place her trust in Christ in her home in Wales. He has given me so much!

He has given me strength in time of trouble. When my three oldest teenagers rebelled against Him, He

92

showed me through His Word that I should accept them, love them, and pray for them as they were. And that I should praise Him for His promise that says, "I will contend with him that contendeth with thee and I will save thy children."

And wouldn't you know it, that's exactly what He's doing. He's a wonderful Saviour. Amen.

*Nickie Stansberry is the dean of women at Aldersgate Free Methodist College in Moose Jaw, Saskatchewan. She also serves as soloist in summer conventions and church crusades.*

Other HORIZON HOUSE books
you will immensely enjoy

*MY GOD CAN DO ANYTHING by Clarence Shrier* is an amazing account of God's healing intervention in one man's life. Some stories are just incredible—this one is true. 96 pages, paper, $1.50.

*TALL TALES THAT ARE TRUE by British Columbia Storyteller Arthur H. Townsend.* A fascinating collection of crisply-written short stories with spiritual applications. **A Million-Dollar Bonfire, The Pig Was Insured,** *and many others. An excellent gift. 96 pages, paper, $1.50.*

*BEYOND THE TANGLED MOUNTAIN by Douglas C. Percy* is an authentic African novel by an award-winning Canadian author. From his pen spins a fascinating web of missionary heroism, romance, tension and tragedy. Douglas Percy is one of the "best" on Africa. First time in paperback. 160 pages, paper, $1.95.

*THE VALLEY OF SHADOWS by Jake Plett is the chronicle of one man's agony. His wife Mary Ann, a pert and pretty real estate saleslady, was abducted and murdered near Edmonton, Alberta. There were no clues. The remains were hidden under the winter snows. And while Jake Plett and his two small sons waited, they took a spiritual pilgrimage. Inspiring reading, excellent for a gift. 133 pages, paper, $1.75.*

*CHOCOLATE CAKE AND ONIONS... WITH LOVE by Marilynne E. Foster is a collection of recipes that she has discovered in her own use to be tasty and easy to prepare. The love comes in selected excerpts from many writings about the theme of love. 96 pages, spiral spine, paper, $1.75.*

*Ask for these books from your bookseller. Or order them directly from HORIZON HOUSE PUBLISHERS, Box 600, Beaverlodge, Alberta, Canada. Please include 15 cents for postage and handling for each book ordered.*

# DON'T MISS
## THESE CURRENT
### Bantam Bestsellers

## ABOUT THE AUTHOR

JAMES HERRIOT is still a practicing veterinary surgeon. He grew up in Scotland and went to Glasgow Veterinary College. After qualifying he went to work in the Yorkshire Dales of northern England. Except for wartime service in the R.A.F., he has never left Yorkshire, and he still works with Siegfried and Tristan Farnon, the colorful characters in *All Creatures Great and Small* and *ALL THINGS BRIGHT AND BEAUTIFUL.* Outside his work, his interests are music, football and dog-walking. James Herriot is married, with a son who is a veterinary surgeon and a daughter who is a doctor.